CW01083985

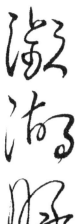

THE LAKESIDE MASTER'S STUDY OF THE PULSE

by Li Shi-zhen

translated by
Bob Flaws

Published by:

BLUE POPPY PRESS
A Division of Blue Poppy Enterprises, Inc.
5441 Western Ave., #2
BOULDER, CO 80301

First Edition, November, 1998
Second Printing, January, 2002

ISBN 1-891845-01-2

The information in this book is given in good faith. However, the translators and the publishers cannot be held responsible for any error or omission. Nor can they be held in any way responsible for treatment given on the basis of information contained in this book. The publishers make this information available to English language readers for scholarly and research purposes only.

The publishers do not advocate nor endorse self-medication by laypersons. Chinese medicine is a professional medicine. Laypersons interested in availing themselves of the treatments described in this book should seek out a qualified professional practitioner of Chinese medicine.

COMP Designation: Denotative translation

Printed at Johnson Printing, Boulder CO

10 9 8 7 6 5 4 3 2

PREFACE

This book is a translation of Li Shi-zhen's *Bin Hu Mai Xue (The Lakeside Master's Study of the Pulse)*. The first section of this late Ming dynasty book is from Cui Jia-yan's *Si Yan Ju Yao (Gathered Essentials in Four Characters)* written some time circa 479 CE. This was then edited by Li Yanwen, Li Shi-zhen's father. The Chinese original of this first section is written in four word or syllable lines or rhymes. The second section is Li Shi-zhen's further commentary on the descriptions and indications of the 27 main pulses. This section was composed in seven word or seven syllable lines. In many cases, this section is merely the repetition of lines from section one. In other cases, Li adds new material to clarify that found in section one.

Because this book was written in meter and verse, it was meant for memorization, not just reading. Many of the lines in both section one and section two are direct (but unattributed) quotes from various early Chinese medical classics, such as the *Nei Jing (Inner Classic)*, *Nan Jing (Classic of Difficulties)*, *Shang Han Lun/Jin Gui Yao Lue (Treatise on Damage [Due to] Cold)/Essentials of the Golden Cabinet)*, *Mai Jing (Pulse Classic)*, and *Zhu Bing Yuan Hou Lun (Treatise on the Causes & Symptoms of All Diseases)*. Also because this book was written in meter and verse, the author has sometimes used unusual word choices or constructions in order to fit the scheme which he has imposed upon himself.

Due to the ease of memorizing this text and its succinctness, this book has been perennially popular in China from the date of its composition to this. It is one of the seminal texts on Chinese pulse examination in the Chinese medical literature. However, till now, no English language translation of it has been available. The so-called translation published under the title *Li Shi Zhen Pulse Diagnosis* by Paradigm Publications is not a translation of the text but rather a translation of a modern Chinese commentary or explanation of that text. Although this version is very popular in English-speaking (or at least English-reading) countries, it is not an accurate and faithful rendition of this extremely important Chinese medical text.

Because I have long been a student of Chinese pulse examination with a special appreciation for this book, I have attempted to render the text itself into English as an addition to Blue Poppy Press's Great Masters Series. Because this text is essentially poetry, not prose, and in an effort to capture a little of both its flavor as well as meaning, I have tried to maintain its succinctness and brevity. Therefore, the reader will have to supply many connecting words not appearing in the Chinese but necessary if one were writing in fluid English. In places where the meaning is totally opaque without adding more than a few words not in the text, I have added clarifications as footnotes. Where only a few extra words have been necessary to bring out the meaning in English, these extra words have been added in parentheses.

Since there is at least one commentary explaining the clinical meanings and applications of this text already available in English as Paradigm Publications' aforementioned book, I have not included my own commentary herein. Rather, I have created this translation as a research source for other practitioners and Chinese medical scholars to comment on and debate. Therefore, the beginning reader should read this text side by side with Paradigm Publications' version in order to gain a more complete understanding. That being said, I do not necessarily agree with all the interpretations found in Paradigm's version, and the attentive reader of both these books will find discrepancies in interpretation between the two.

The translational terminology used in making this translation is based on Nigel Wiseman's *English-Chinese Chinese-English Dictionary of Chinese Medicine*, Hunan Science & Technology Press, Changsha, 1995. Divergences from this standard are identified and explained in the footnotes. The source texts I used in making this translation were primarily the *Bin Hu Mai Xue Bai Shuo Jie (The Lakeside Master's Study of the Pulse Clearly Explained)* by the Beijing College of Chinese Medicine published by the People's Health & Hygiene Press, Beijing, 1993, and the *Zhong Yi Mai Xue Ru Men (Entering the Gate of the Study of Chinese Medicine's Pulse)* by Jiang Chang-yuan, Science & Technology Literature Publishing Co., Chengdu, 1986. Other sources are listed in the Bibliography at the back of this book.

In premodern Chinese there was no punctuation. Characters were written in columns one after the other. One of the first hurdles in learning to read Chinese in olden days was figuring out where "sentences" stopped and started. I've put the word sentences in parentheses because that concept is an English language one which does not really exist per se in Chinese. To make reading such premodern texts simpler, modern editors have added their own punctuation borrowed from English. However, as soon as you start adding punctuation, you are forcing a certain interpretation on the original which may or may not be what the author intended. In a number of places, I have, therefore, taken the liberty of changing the punctuation as found in contemporary Chinese versions. In a number of places, this does change the meaning of the passage as compared to modern Chinese editions and their commentaries.

Those readers interested in going even deeper into a study of Chinese pulse examination are recommended to see Wang Shu-he's *The Pulse Classic*, a translation of the *Mai Jing* by Yang Shou-zhong, and my *The Secret of Chinese Pulse*

Diagnosis, both also published by Blue Poppy Press. In addition, Blue Poppy Seminars makes available a Distance Learning Program in Chinese Pulse Diagnosis based on audiotapes of my live lectures.

Bob Flaws
Boulder, CO
Nov. 10, 1997

TABLE OF CONTENTS

FOUR WORD RHYMES

Chapter 1
Channel Vessels & Vessel Qi[1]

The pulse is the blood vessels[2]
Which precede the qi and blood.
They are the tunnels of the blood
And respond to the qi respiration.

---

[1]It is not clear to me whether these chapter numbers and headings are part of the original *Bin Hu Mai Xue* or later additions by contemporary editors.

[2] The Chinese word *mai* means both vessels and pulse. In some places, it needs to be translated as vessels, in other places as pulse. However, the Chinese is simply *mai* in all cases. Because of these dual meanings, at least when rendered in English, it is difficult to keep subject and verb number corresponding and consistent. Hopefully the reader will understand that there is more ambiguity in the Chinese or at least *double entendre* than there is in the English translation.

Their image follows the earth.[3]
They are the mansion of the blood.
They unite with the heart
And the skin is their position.[4]

They are supplied beginning from the kidneys.
Their supplies are engendered by the
    stomach.[5]
They are yin within yang
And are rooted in the constructive and
    defensive.

---

[3] This means the appearance of the vessels is modeled on or is like the rivers which run through the earth.

[4] This means the blood vessels unite with the heart internally, while they are located within the skin externally.

[5] In other words, the blood which flows in the vessels has its source in both the former heaven kidneys and latter heaven spleen and stomach.

The constructive is all the yin and blood.
The defensive is all the yang and qi.
The constructive moves internally (and/or
    within) the vessels.
The defensive moves externally (and/or out-
    side) the vessels.[6]

The pulse (or vessels) does not move by itself.
It follows the qi and arrives.
The qi stirs and the pulse (or vessels) respond,
Yin and yang in relationship.

---

[6] Most translations of these two lines merely say the
constructive moves within the vessels, while the defensive
moves outside the vessels. However, the words *nei* and *wai*
also mean internal and external when speaking
anatomically in a Chinese medical sense. Certainly, when it
comes to the defensive qi, this second meaning, that it
moves in the external part of the body, is equally as
important as the fact that it flows outside the vessels.

3

Qi is like a bellows.
Blood is like billows.
Blood vessels, qi respiration,
Ascension and descension equal circulation.

Within the 12 channels,
All have stirring vessels.[7]
(However,) only hand *tai yin*,
The inch mouth, is chosen to determine them
    all.

This channel homes to the lungs,
Above tying with the throat.
It is the great meeting of the vessels
(Where) respiration exits and enters.

---

[7] Stirring vessels means palpable pulses. In other words, one
can feel various pulses on each of the 12 channels.

One inhalation, one exhalation,
Four (beats) arriving is normal flow.
(One) day and night, ten thousand
Three thousand five hundred (beats).[8]

One inhalation, one exhalation,
The pulse moves six *cun*.
(One) day and night, eight hundred
Ten *zhang* is the norm.[9]

---

[8] *I.e.,* in 24 hours, the pulse beats normally 13,500 times.

[9] One *zhang* equals 3 ½ meters.

Chapter 2
POSITIONS (&) DIAGNOSTIC METHODS

One begins by holding the pulse,
Holding the palm face upward.
Behind the palm (is) a high bone.
It is called the bar ascending.

In front of the bar is yang.
Behind the bar is yin.
Yang, inch; yin, cubit.
First and later, push and search.[10]

---

[10] This means one should sequentially push and search through each of these different positions in a systematic way.

(If) inch mouth, no pulse,
(Then) investigate the outer wrist.
This is called opposite bar.
This is not sufficient for blame.[11]

Heart and liver reside on the left.
Lungs and spleen reside on the right.
Kidneys and life gate
Reside at both cubit positions.

Left is the human's prognosis.
Right is the qi mouth.
The spirit gate makes a decision.
It is located behind the bar on both (hands).[12]

---

[11] This means that an opposite bar pulse should not be taken as a pathological indication.

[12] The spirit gate is the name the *Mai Jing (Pulse Classic)* gives to both cubit positions when these are used to assess the body's root and prognosis.

(When) humans do not (have these)
   two pulses,
Disease and death cannot be stemmed.
Left large is auspicious (or normal) for a man.
Right large is auspicious for a woman.

Men's and women's pulses are the same.
Only the cubit is different.
(If) is yang is weak and yin is exuberant,
Contrarily, disease arrives.[13]

The pulse has seven examinations.
These are called floating, middle, and deep.
Above, below, right and left.
These bits of information are sought
   and searched.

---

[13] Here the author is talking about the situation in males. The reverse of this obtains in women. Yang refers to the inch, while yin refers to the cubit.

There are also nine indicators:
Lifting, pressing, light and heavy,
Three positions, floating and deep.
Each is sought for five stirrings.[14]

The inch indicates the chest and upper (body).
The bar indicates below the diaphragm.
The cubit indicates below the navel
Down to the heels and ankles.

The left pulse indicates the left.
The right pulse indicates the right.
(If) there is disease, follow its location.
(If) no disease, there isn't any.[15]

---

[14] If one searches for five beats in each of the three positions at each of three depths, these are the nine indicators.

[15] In other words, if one is diseased, look for its manifestation in the corresponding pulse position. If there is no disease, there will not be any particular pathological signs in any pulse positions.

Chapter 3
FIVE VISCERA LEVEL NORMAL[16] PULSES

Floating is the heart and lungs.
Sunken is the kidneys and liver.
The spleen and stomach central islet[17]
Are between floating and deep.

The heart pulse is floating,
Floating, large, and scattered.
The lung pulse is floating,
Floating, choppy, and short.

---

[16] The word for normal here is ping which literally means level denotatively and calm connotatively.

[17] Central islet is another name for the middle burner.

The liver pulse is sunken,
Sunken, long, and bowstring.[18]
The kidney pulse is sunken,
Sunken, replete, and soft.

The spleen and stomach pulse
In general should be harmonious and
     moderate.
(For) life gate and source yang,
Both cubits are judged together.

---

[18] Wiseman suggests stringlike pulse for *xian mai*. He argues
that the Chinese did not have the technology to make wire
at the time that this word was coined. Be that as it may,
the Chinese character clearly shows the picture of a
tightly drawn bowstring, not simply a limp string. In
addition, Chinese-English dictionaries either define this
character as bowstring or like a taut string of an instrument,
such as a zither, dulcimer, or lute. Therefore, I agree with
Wiseman that wiry pulse is not right, but I prefer bowstring
over stringlike since the tense quality is absolutely
fundamental to understanding and being able to feel this
pulse.

Spring, bowstring; summer, surging;
Fall, hair(-like); winter, stone(-like).[19]
(If, in) the four seasons, harmonious and
    moderate,
This is called a level (or normal) pulse.

If greatly excessive, replete and strong,
Disease is engendered in the external.
If not reaching, vacuous and faint,
Disease is engendered in the internal.

In the four times (*i.e.*, seasons) there may be
    hundreds of diseases,
(Nevertheless,) the stomach qi supports the
    root.
A pulse which is highly valued has spirit.

---

[19]Hair-like is interpreted as floating, soft, and vacuous, while
stone-like is interpreted as deep and forceful.

It is not ok not to examine (for these).[20]

---

[20] This verse means that, no matter what disease there may be whenever during the year, one must assess whether there is stomach qi, root, and spirit. Root refers to the kidneys, while spirit refers to a moderate quality within the pulse. The pulse may be a certain diseased image, but it should not be solely that image. It should still have some size, some strength, and it should not be completely tight or tense.

Chapter 4
PULSE DISCRIMINATION OUTLINE

(One must) regulate and collect their own qi,
Inhaling and exhaling with stable respiration.[21]
Four arrivals, five arrivals,
Normal flow is level and harmonious.[22]

Three arrivals is slow.
Slow is made by chill.
Six arrivals is rapid.
Rapidity evidences a heat condition.

---

[21] The word stable not only means at fixed, steady intervals but also implies calm. Here, the author is referring to the practitioner's qi.

[22] The word level means calm but also means something level in space, *i.e.*, with no high and lows. A normal pulse beats 4-5 times per respiration.

Changing to slow (is) changing to chill.
Changing to rapid (is) changing to heat.
Slow and rapid must be (made) clear.
Floating and sunken should be differentiated.

Floating and sunken, slow and rapid
Discriminate internal and external causes.
External is due to heaven.
Internal is due to humans.

Heaven has yin, yang,
Wind, rain, darkness, and brightness.
Humans (have) joy, anger, anxiety,
Thought, sorrow, fear, and fright.

(If) external causes result in floating
This is due to exterior patterns.
Sunken, internal; slow, yin.
Rapidity is yang exuberance.

If internal causes result in floating,
This is the presence of vacuity wind.
Sunken, qi; slow, chill.
Rapidity, heat. Who can doubt (this)?

Floating and rapid, exterior heat.
Sunken and rapid, interior heat.
Floating and slow, exterior vacuity.
Sunken and slow, chilling and binding.

Exterior, interior, yin, and yang,
Wind, qi, chill, and heat.
To discriminate internal and external causes,
Consult and differentiate the pulse
    and conditions.[23]

---

[23] In other words, one must compare and contrast the pulse
and the other symptoms before arriving at a diagnosis. One
should not proceed on the basis of the pulse alone.

Pulse principles are vast and numerous,
(But they can) be summed up in four.
Since (we) have obtained the outline,
(We can) extend (their meaning) to strike the
    (other) varieties.[24]

---

[24] The first three characters in this line show a bow and arrow, a target, and then the third character which means to touch, to contact, to hit, or to strike. Therefore, there is a pictographic analogy here which is more visual than our translation conveys.

Chapter 5
THE FORMS & APPEARANCES OF ALL THE PULSES

The floating pulse is modeled on heaven.
A light hand and it can be obtained.
Floating, floating,[25] located above,
Like wood drifting on water.

---

[25] The two words here rendered floating are *fan fan*. They mean floating but are not the same word as floating pulse (*fu mai*). As a compound term, *fan fan* means *not* deep.

(If it) has force, (it is) surging and large.
It comes exuberant and departs long and
  drawn-out.[26]
(If it) has no force, (it is) vacuous and large.
It is slow and also soft.

If extremely vacuous, it is scattered.
It melts and overflows without restraint.[27]

(If it) has force (but) is without center,
This is called scallion-stalk.
The scallion-stalk is tense and bowstring.
The drumskin pulse is even more so.

---

[26] Long and drawn out is a single Chinese word, *you*. Other
Chinese texts say the surging pulse comes exuberant and
departs long (*chang*). However, *you* also means leisurely. So
this might be rendered as comes exuberant and departs
leisurely or slowly.

[27] It is sometimes explained in Chinese sources that the
scattered pulse has no edges.

Floating and small and also soft,[28]
(Like) a thread floating on the face of water.
(If) extremely soft, is faint.
Does not assume its post when searched and
    pressed.

Sunken is modeled on earth.
It is near to the sinews and bones.
Sunken, sunken, it is located beneath.
(If) extremely sunken, it is deep-lying.

(If it) has force, it is confined,
Replete, large, bowstring, and long.
(If) extremely confined, this is replete,
Driving, driving[29] and strong.

---

[28] Here soft is both an attribute and one of the proper names
of this pulse, the soft pulse or *ruan mai*.

[29] This could also be rendered as beating, beating.

(If it) is forceless, it is weak,
Soft and small like a thread.
(If) extremely weak, it is fine
Like a (single) silk thread.

The slow pulse is categorized as yin.
One respiration, three arrivals.
A little (more) rapid than slow,
Moderate (*i.e.*, relaxed) is capable of reaching
    by four (beats).[30]

---

[30] Wiseman gives moderate pulse for *huan mai*. That is ok
with me when this pulse name described a normal, healthy
pulse. However, when this name describes a diseased pulse,
as it most often does, I believe it is better to say that it is
relaxed or slack. Most often, this means that it is slightly
slow in its numbers of arrivals per respiration. Therefore, I
have included the words relaxed and sometimes even
slightly slow in parentheses after each time the moderate
pulse is mentioned in order to underscore the connotative
meaning as opposed to the denotative name.

Two (beats or) less, one defeat,
A disease which cannot be treated.
Two breaths (one beat), wrested essence,
The pulse already has no qi.

Slow and fine is choppy.
It pours and comes with extreme difficulty.
It appears to stop but doesn't stop.
It is both short and scattered simultaneously.

Bound comes moderate (*i.e.*, relaxed or slightly
    slow).
It stops and then resumes its coming.
The regularly interrupted comes moderate
    (*i.e.*, slightly slow).
It stops and is not able to recover.

The rapid pulse is categorized as yang.
Six arrivals, one respiration.
Seven is racing, eight is extreme.
Nine arrivals is desertion.

Pouring and coming flowingly and
    uninhibitedly,
This is called slippery.
(If it) has force, it is tight.
It is pellet-like like a rope.[31]

If rapid appears at the inch mouth
And has a stop, this is skipping.
If rapid appears at the bar center,
A stirring pulse can be indicated.
It stirs and it shakes (or waves).
Its form is like a bean.

Long is qi punishing.[32]
It exceeds its position.
Long and extremely straight,
The bowstring pulse responds to the fingers.

---

[31] Pellet-like means both hard and round like a ball or pellet. This word has since become one name for a bullet or a pill.

[32] Meaning chaos or counterflow.

Short is qi disease.

It is unable to fill its position.

It does not appear in the bar.

It only indicates the cubit and inch.[33]

---

[33] In other words, the short pulse is only seen in the bar. It does not extend to the cubit and inch. Therefore, the short pulse is not short in the bar, but only short in the cubit and inch where it is absent.

Chapter 6
THE MAIN DISEASES
OF ALL THE PULSES

One pulse, one form.
Each has its main diseases.
(Depending on which are) mutually simulta-
neous (with) the rapid pulse,[34]
One sees various conditions.

Floating pulse, mainly exterior.
The interior must be insufficient.
(If it) has force, wind heat.
No force, blood weakness.

---

[34] In other words, depending on which other pulses are combined with the rapid pulse...

Floating and slow, wind vacuity.

Floating and rapid, wind heat.

Floating and tight, wind cold.

Floating and moderate (*i.e.*, relaxed), wind
  dampness.

Floating and vacuous, damage by summerheat.

Floating and scallion-stalk, loss of blood.

Floating and surging, vacuity fire.

Floating and faint, extreme taxation.

Floating and soft, yin vacuity.

Floating and scattered, acute (or intense)
  vacuity.

Floating and bowstring, phlegm rheum.

Floating and slippery, phlegm heat.

Sunken pulse, mainly interior,

Mainly cold, mainly accumulation.

(If it) has force, phlegm food.

No force, qi depression.

Sunken and slow, vacuity cold.
Sunken and rapid, heat deep-lying.
Sunken and tight, chilly pain.
Sunken and moderate (or relaxed),
   water amassment.

Sunken and confined, inveterate chill.
Sunken and replete, extreme heat.
Sunken and weak, yin vacuity.
Sunken and fine, impediment dampness.

Sunken and bowstring, rheum pain.
Sunken and slippery, long-standing food.
Sunken and deep-lying, vomiting and
   disinhibition (*i.e.*, diarrhea),
Yin toxins gathering and accumulation.

Slow pulse, mainly viscera.
Yang qi deep-lying and hidden.
(If it) has force, there is pain.
No force, vacuity cold.

Rapid pulse, mainly heat,
Mainly vomiting, mainly the bowels.
Has force, there is heat.
No force, there are sores.

Slippery pulse, mainly phlegm
Or damage by food.
Below there is amassment of blood.
Above there is vomiting counterflow.

Choppy pulse, scanty blood
Or central cold and dampness,
Contrary stomach (*i.e.*, nausea), bound
    intestines,
Spontaneous perspiration, reversal
    counterflow.

Bowstring pulse, mainly rheum,
Diseases pertaining to the gallbladder and
    liver.
Bowstring and rapid, mostly heat.
Bowstring and slow, mostly cold.[35]

Floating and bowstring, branch rheum.
Sunken and bowstring, suspended pain.
Yang bowstring, headache.
Yin bowstring, abdominal pain.[36]

Tight pulse, mainly cold,
Also mainly all (types of) pain.
Floating and tight, exterior cold.
Sunken and tight, interior pain.

---

[35] These two lines might also be translated as a lot of heat and a lot of cold, or excessive heat, excessive cold respectively.

[36] Yin and yang here mean cubit and inch respectively.

Long pulse, qi level. [37]
Short pulse, qi disease.
Fine is scanty qi.
Large is disease moving forward.

Floating and long, wind epilepsy.
Sunken and short, long-standing food.
Blood vacuity, a vacuous pulse.
Qi repletion, a replete pulse.

A surging pulse is heat.
Its yin is vacuous.
A fine pulse is dampness.
Its blood is vacuous.

---

[37] Here the long pulse means that the qi is normal, as opposed to the next pulse which indicates that the qi is diseased.

Moderate (or relaxed) and large, all wind.

Moderate (or relaxed) and fine, all dampness.

Moderate (or relaxed) and choppy, blood scanty.

Moderate (or relaxed) and slippery, internal heat.

Soft and small, yin vacuity.

Weak and small, yang vacuity.

Yang exhausted, aversion to cold,

Yin vacuity, effusion of heat (or fever).

Yang faint, aversion to cold.

Yin faint, effusion of heat.[38]

Males faint, vacuity detriment.

Females faint, draining of blood.

---

[38] Effusion of heat might be and usually is translated more simply as fever. However, it literally means that heat is emitted or effused to the external part of the body. There is no concept of fever per se in traditional Chinese medicine.

Yang stirring, exiting of sweat.
Yin stirring, effusion of heat,
Pain or fright,
Flooding strike, loss of blood.

Vacuity and cold mutually wrestle,
This is called drumskin.
Men's loss of essence,
Women's loss of blood.

Yang exuberance leads to skipping.
Lung abscess, yang evils.
Yin exuberance leads to binding.
Mounting, concretions, accumulations, and
    depression.

Regularly interrupted, qi debility
Or diarrhea with pus and blood,
Damage due to cold, heart palpitations,
Women's fetus three months.[39]

---

[39] In other words, this pulse may correspond to a three month pregnancy.

Chapter 7
MISCELLANEOUS DISEASES[40]
PULSE IMAGES

(In terms of) the main diseases of the pulse,
There are appropriate and inappropriate
　　(varieties).
Yin and yang may flow normally or　counter-
flow.[41]
Inauspicious and auspicious can be inferred.

---

[40] Miscellaneous diseases do not mean left-over or supernumerary. This is simply the term used in Chinese medicine for all the usual diseases enumerated in the treatment sections of Chinese medical books.

[41] This means that the pathological changes due to interrelationships between yin and yang may be normal or abnormal, expected or unexpected, auspicious or inauspicious.

Wind stroke (should be) floating and moderate
(or relaxed).
(If) tense and replete, abstain.[42]
Floating and slippery, phlegm stroke.
Sunken and slow, qi stroke.

Corpse reversal, sunken and slippery,
Dying, not knowing people.
Entering the viscus, bodily chill.
Entering the bowels, bodily warmth.[43]

Wind damaging the defensive,
Floating and moderate (or relaxed), has
sweating.
Cold damaging the constructive,
Floating and tight, no sweating.

---

[42] The Chinese, *ji*, means fear, dread, abstain, scruple, avoid, and shun. It implies both a bad prognosis and suggests that the doctor should not try to treat this patient for fear they will be blamed when the patient dies.

[43] Stroke may be categorized as either being in the viscera or in the bowels.

Summerheat damaging the qi,
The pulse is vacuous and there's bodily heat.
Dampness damaging the blood,
The pulse is moderate (or relaxed), fine, and
  choppy.

Damage by cold, heat disease,
The pulse tends to be floating and surging.
Sunken and faint, choppy and small,
The condition contrarily must be inauspicious.

(If,) after sweating, the pulse is still,
The body is cool, this leads to quiet.
(If,) after sweating, the pulse is agitated,
Heat is severe, this must be difficult (to treat).

Drink and food internally damaging,
The qi mouth is tense and slippery.
Taxation fatigue internally damaging,
The spleen pulse is large and weak.

(If) longing for knowledge has affected the qi[44],
Under the hand the pulse is sunken.
If extremely sunken, this is deep-lying,
Choppy and weak, enduringly deep.

Fire depression is mostly sunken.
Slippery is phlegm, tight is food.
Qi, choppy; blood, scallion-stalk.
Rapid, fire; fine, dampness.

Slippery is mainly profuse phlegm.
Bowstring is mainly lodged rheum.
Heat leads to slippery and rapid.
Cold leads to bowstring and tight.

Floating and simultaneously slippery, wind.
Sunken and simultaneously slippery, qi.
Food damage, short and racing.
Damp lodging, soft and fine.

---

[44] In old China, students studying for their Confucian
examinations often caused themselves internal damage due
to excessive taxation and overfatigue.

The malaria pulse appears bowstring.[45]
Bowstring and rapid, all heat.
Bowstring and slow, all cold.
Regularly interrupted and scattered, all
     turning back.[46]

Discharge, draining, precipitation, dysentery,[47]
Sunken, small, slippery, weak.
Replete, large, floating, and surging,
Effusion of heat leads to a malign (outcome).

---

[45] Malaria here simply means any disease with alternating fever and chills. This is malaria-like disease but not necessarily the same Western medical named disease.

[46] Or about to break, *i.e.*, about to die

[47] In other words, diarrhea and dysentery

Vomiting and contrary stomach (*i.e.*, nausea),
Floating and slippery, all flourishing (*i.e.*, an ok
   prognosis).
Bowstring, rapid, tight, choppy,
Bound intestines, all perishing.

Cholera-like indications,
The pulse is regularly interrupted, no surprise.
Reversal counterflow, slow and faint,
This is (something) one can fear.

Coughing, mostly floating,
Gathering in the stomach barring the lungs.
Sunken, tight, small, danger.
Floating and soft, easily treated.

Panting, rapid breathing with (lifted)
   shoulders,
Floating and slippery, all are normal (or
   auspicious).
Sunken and choppy, limbs cold,
Scattered pulse, inauspicious condition.[48]

Disease heat, have fire,
Surging and rapid, can be doctored.
Sunken and faint, no fire,
No root, all dangerous.

Bone steaming effusion of heat,
Pulse rapid and also vacuous.
Heat and also choppy and small,
Must relinquish this human body.

---

[48] Inauspicious here, *ni*, could also be translated as
counterflow. Panting and cough are counterflow
conditions. So, although the meaning is mostly that the
prognosis is bad, the choice of words is still a bit of a *double
entendre*.

Taxation extreme, all vacuous.
Floating, soft, faint, and weak.
Spleen vanquished, both (hands) bowstring,
Fire flaming, tense and rapid.[49]

(In) all pathological losses of blood,
The pulse must appear scallion-stalk.
Moderate (or relaxed) and small, can be happy.
Rapid and large, can be anxious.

Static blood internally amassed,
Nevertheless should be confined and large.
Sunken, small, choppy, and faint,
Contrarily produces disaster.

---

[49] Liver yang hyperactivity and exuberance may damage the spleen and stomach, thus giving rise to yin vacuity and yang hyperactivity. Thus the pulse is tense and rapid.

Emission of essence and white turbidity[50],
Faint, choppy, and also weak.
Large and exuberant, yin vacuity,
Scallion-stalk, soft, surging, and rapid.

(In terms of) the pulses of the three wastings[51],
(If) floating and large, all live.
Fine, small, faint, and choppy,
Formal desertion can (be cause for) fright.

Urinary dribbling and block,
Nose head colored yellow,
Choppy and small, no blood.
Rapid and large, what obstruction?

---

[50] White turbidity refers to involuntary emission of semen when urinating.

[51] The three wastings are upper, middle, and lower wasting. These refer to cachetic disease with emaciation. Commonly, the three wastings correspond to various types of diabetes.

Stools dry and bound.
The form (of the pulse) is divided into qi and
    blood.
Yang (constipation) may be faint or replete.[52]
Yin (constipation) may be slow and choppy.

Withdrawal is heavy (or double) yin.
Mania is heavy yang (or double) yang.
Floating and surging is auspicious.
Sunken and tense is inauspicious.

The epilepsy pulse should be vacuous.
Replete and tense, all are malign.
Floating is yang (epilepsy); sunken is yin
    (epilepsy).
Phlegm, slippery; rapid, heat.

---

[52] Most Chinese explanations of this line say that yang
constipation mostly exhibits a fast and replete or sunken
and replete pulse. No mention is made of faint. This may be
a typographical error, although it does appear in several
contemporary Chinese versions.

(In terms of) the pulse of throat impediment,
Rapid, heat; slow, cold.
In galloping horse throat entwining[53],
Faint and deep-lying leads to difficulties.

All wind, vertigo and dizziness.
(Can also) have fire, have phlegm.
Left choppy, dead blood.
Right large, vacuity can be read.

Head pain, mostly bowstring.
Floating, wind; tight, cold;
Heat, surging; dampness, fine.
Moderate (or relaxed), summerheat; slippery,
    phlegm.

Qi vacuity, bowstring and soft.
Blood vacuity, faint and choppy.
Kidney reversal, bowstring and hard.
True pain, short and choppy.

---

[53] *I.e.*, very sudden, very acute throat impediment, usually
due to liver-spleen accumulated fire.

Pain of the heart and abdomen,
It has nine types.
Fine and slow, healing is speedy.
Floating and large, the course is enduring.

Mounting qi, bowstring and tense,
Accumulations and gatherings located in the
   interior.
Drumskin and tense, all live.
Weak and tense, all die.

The pulses of low back pain
Mostly are deep and bowstring.
(If) simultaneously floating, all wind.
(If) simultaneously tight, all cold.

Bowstring, and slippery, phlegm rheum.
Soft and fine, kidneys may be read.
Large is kidney vacuity.
Deep and replete, twisted muscles.[54]

Foot qi has four (types).
Slow, cold; rapid, heat;
Floating and slippery, all wind;
Soft and fine, all dampness.

Wilting disease lung vacuity,
The pulse is mostly fine and moderate (or
    relaxed).
Possibly choppy, possibly tight.
Possibly fine, possibly soft.

---

[54] The Chinese word *na* which I have translated as muscles here is not in any of my Chinese-English dictionaries by itself. Chinese texts gloss the term as the muscles and flesh of the low back region. The word twisted also means to sprain, to dodge, or to flash. Implied, therefore, is injury to the low back due to sudden wrenching movement which also causes flashes of acute pain.

Wind cold damp qi
(May) combine to form impediment.
Floating, choppy, and also tight,
(These) three pulses may have.

The five jaundices, replete heat.
The pulse must be surging and rapid.
Choppy and faint is categorized as vacuity.
Surely dread (if there is) a feeling of thirst.[55]

(If) the pulses obtained are all sunken,
Ask of them if they have water (*i.e.*, swelling).
(In that case,) floating (is) qi or wind.
Sunken (is) stone or interior.

---

[55] The word dread in this line also means to shun, avoid, or scruple. Thus the prognosis in this case is poor and the doctor should consider avoiding this case for fear of being blamed when the patient dies.

Sunken and rapid is yang.
Sunken and slow is yin.
Floating and large, can control.
Vacuous and small, can (cause) fright.

Long, full, pulse bowstring,
The spleen contracts liver tyranny.[56]
Damp heat, rapid and surging.
Yin cold, slow and weak.

Floating is vacuity fullness.
Tight is center repletion.
Floating and large, can treat.
Vacuous and small, extreme danger.

The five viscera (may) have accumulations.
The six bowels (may) have gatherings.
Replete and strong, all light.
Sunken and fine, all severe.

---

[56] Spleen earth is controlled by liver wood.

Nausea and abdominal distention,
Tight and fine, all live.
If the pulse is floating and large,
Evil qi is already sunk deep.

Welling and flat abscesses, floating and
    scattered,
Aversion to cold, effusion of heat.
If have pain in a (certain) location,
Welling or flat abscesses will emit there.

Pulse rapid and effusion of heat
Along with pain, all yang.
Not rapid, no heat.
No aching, yin sores.

Unruptured welling or flat abscesses,
No fear (if) surging and large.
Already ruptured welling or flat abscesses,
Floating and large, can fear.

Lung abscess already produced,
Inch rapid and also replete.
Lung wilting of form,
Rapid and also forceless.

Lung abscess, color (*i.e.*, complexion) white,
The pulse should be short and choppy.
It should not be floating and large.
(In that case,) spittle (is like) plaster, vomiting
    blood.

Intestinal abscess, replete heat,
Slippery and rapid can be known.
Rapid but also no heat,
Bar pulse scallion-stalk and vacuous.

Faint, choppy, and also tight,
No pus, should precipitate.
Tight, rapid, pus formed,
Surely one cannot precipitate.

Chapter 8
WOMEN & CHILDREN'S PULSE METHODS

Women's pulses,
Take blood as the root.
(If) blood is effulgent, (they) easily (get with)
    fetus (*i.e.*, conceive).
(If) qi is effulgent, pregnancy (is) difficult.

(If) the *shao yin* is especially stirring,
This is called having a child.
Cubit pulse slippery and uninhibited,
Pregnant, can be joyful.

Slippery, racing, and also scattered[57],
Fetus must be three months.
However, if racing and not scattered,
It must be five months.

Left racing is a boy.
Right racing is a girl.
A female, the abdomen is like a winnowing
    basket.
A male, the abdomen is like a cauldron.

---

[57] The original text says not scattered. Later editors have corrected this error based on a line from the *Mai Jing (Pulse Classic)* which reads, "Pulse slippery, racing, heavy hand pressure scatters all, fetus already three months." The following lines seem to corroborate that this was a typographical error.

The pulse of longing to birth[58]
Arrives departing from the classics.[59]
Water is precipitated, therefore birth.
Not precipitated, no fright.[60]

The pulse of the newly birthed,
(If) moderate (or relaxed) and slippery is
   auspicious.
Replete, large, bowstring, or confined,
The condition is counterflow (or inauspicious).

---

[58] *I.e.,* being about to give birth

[59] Departing from the classics means unorthodox. It means that the pulse changes slightly from normal.

[60] There is no need for fright or apprehension because birthing has not begun as long as the waters have not broken.

The pulse of children,
Seven arrivals is level (or normal).
Even more (importantly), scrutinize the color
   and symptoms
And read the tiger's mouth.[61]

---

[61] In other words, pulse examination is not as important in infants and small children as in adults. In small children, place more importance on their facial complexion, their symptoms, and examining the three bars at the tiger's mouth. This refers to small visible venules on the palmar surface of the index finger at the metacarpal-phalangeal joint, the proximal interphalangeal joint, and the distal interphalangeal joint. For more information on this form of pediatric diagnosis, see my *A Handbook of TCM Pediatrics*, Blue Poppy Press, 1997.

Chapter 9
EXTRAORDINARY CHANNELS EIGHT VESSELS PULSE EXAMINATION METHODS

(In terms of) the extraordinary channels eight
    vessels[62],
Their examination (is) yet different.
Straight up, straight down,
Floating is the governing (vessel).

---

[62] In Chinese, the full name of the eight extraordinary
vessels is the extraordinary channels eight vessels.

Confined is the penetrating (vessel).
Tight is the conception (vessel).[63]
Inch left (to) right, pellet-like[64],
Yang qiao can be determined.

Cubit left (to) right, pellet-like,
Yin qiao can be differentiated.
Bar left (to) right, pellet-like,
Dai mai should be knacked.[65]

---

[63] Wiseman gives controlling vessel for *ren mai*. Since conception is a correct alternative rendition of *ren* and this term has been universally accepted within the profession, I see no sense in bucking the tide on this term.

[64] Pellet-like means both round and hard. However, it does not imply short.

[65] Knack also means trick of the trade. In English, neither of these terms is a verb. In Chinese, the distinction between nouns and verbs is not so clear. Therefore, I apologize for this infelicitous neologism.

Cubit outer slanting upward,
Arrives (at) the inch, *yin wei*.
Cubit inner slanting upward, arrives (at) the
inch, *yang wei*.

(If) the governing vessel is diseased,
Upper back stiffness, withdrawal and mania.
(If) the conception vessel is diseased,
The seven mountings, concretions and
hardness.

(If) the penetrating vessel is diseased,
Counterflow qi, interior tension.
The *dai* rules *dai xia*[66],
Navel pain, essence loss.

---

[66] *Dai xia* literally means below the belt but figuratively has
come to mean abnormal vaginal discharge.

Yang wei, cold and heat,
Ocular vertigo, stiffness (and/or numbness)
    and falling.
Yin wei, heart pain,
Chest and rib-side piercing and pounding.[67]

(If) the *yang qiao* is diseased,
Yang is relaxed, yin is tense.[68]
(If) the *yin qiao* is diseased,
Yin is relaxed, yang is tense.

Withdrawal and mania, tugging and
    slackening,
Cold and heat, abstraction,
Eight vessels pulses and symptoms,
Each has their affiliation.

---

[67] The word *zhu* in this line means to build or construct and, by extension, to pound. Therefore, there can also be heart palpitations.

[68] In other words, the muscles on the inside of the lower leg are tense and contracted, while the muscles on the outside of the lower leg as relaxed and flaccid.

Chapter 10
TRUE VISCERAL EXPIRY PULSES

Since disease pulses have already (been made)
    clear,
Auspicious and inauspicious should be
    differentiated.
(There are) the channels and vessels in the
    external.
One also has the true vessels (or pulses).

The liver expiry pulse
(It is like) following (*i.e.*, feeling the edge of)
    a knife, punishing, punishing.[69]
The heart expiry pulse
Passes like a bean, agitated and racing.

---

[69] Punishing, punishing is explained in modern Chinese
commentaries as hard and tense.

The spleen is sparrow pecking,
(Or) like a housetop leaking.
Like water flowing,
Like an overturned cup.[70]

Lung expiry, (the pulse is) like hair,
Is without root, bleak and desolate,
(Like) hemp seed stirring and shaking (or
    waving).
It is equal to floating and waving.

The kidney pulse about to expire
Arrives like a visiting guest.
It comes like a pellet (or) stone.
It departs like an unraveling rope.

---

[70] *I.e.*, slowly dripping drop by drop

The destiny[71] pulse about to expire
(Is like) shrimp swimming (or) fish hovering.[72]
(If) it arrives like a gushing spring,
Expiry is located in the bladder.

(In the case of) true pulses no matter which
  form,
The stomach already (has) no qi.
By comparing and scrutinizing the pulse and
  the symptoms.
These can thus be determined easily.

---

[71] The word *ming* is usually translated as life, but its means more than just life. It means life destiny. However, here, it refers to the life gate.

[72] The first analogy implies that the pulse is floating with a sudden jump now and then. The second analogy implies that the pulse is floating at the cubit but cannot be felt at the inch.

(If, in) yang disease, yin appears,
The disease must be dangerous .
(If, in) yin disease, yang appears,
Even so, no calamity.

Above, does not arrive at the bar[73],
Yin qi already expired.
Below, does not arrive at the bar[74],
Yang qi is already exhausted.

A deep-lying pulse stopping to rest,
Viscera expired, collapse, danger.[75]
Scattered pulse, no root.
Formal detriment, difficult to doctor.

---

[73] In other words, a pulse at only the cubit position

[74] In other words, a pulse at only the inch position

[75] This line might also be translated, "Viscera expired tending to danger." It means there is immanent danger of collapse due to visceral expiry.

Seven Word Rhymes

(Under the name of each pulse, there are descriptions of each pulse's shape. These are not written in seven syllable or seven word lines. The seven syllable lines begin below under the section titled Physical Shape Poem. Under each pulse, there are differing numbers of poems or rhymes. In some cases there are physical shape poems, appraising the types poems, and main diseases poems. In other cases, either the physical shape poems are combined with the appraising the types poem or the appraising the types poem is combined with the main diseases poem.)

FLOATING PULSE

Floating pulse, lift and it has a surplus.
Press and it becomes insufficient.[76]
It is like a faint wind blowing over the hairs
    (*i.e.*, feathers) on the back of a bird,
Press, press, whisper, whisper.
It is like an elm pod.[77]
It is like wood floating on top of water.
It is like twisting (*i.e.*, pressing) an onion stalk
    leaf.

Physical Shape Poem

Floating pulse only is plentiful moving above
    the flesh.
It is like an elm pod; it is similar to soft hair.

---

[76] These two lines are from Wang Shu-he's *Mai Jing (Pulse Classic)*.

[77] This simile is from the *Su Wen (Simple Questions)*.

In the three (months of) fall obtain it
  and know there is no ailment.
In enduring disease, come upon it and there
  can be fright!

Appraising[78] the Types Poem

Floating is like wood floating in water.
Floating, large, empty in the center is scallion-
  stalk.
Beating, beating and also floating is the
  surging pulse.
Although when it comes it is exuberant, it
  departs long and drawn out.

A floating pulse soft and level like twisting
  an onion stalk,

---

[78] The word *xiang* when pronounced in one tone means mutual, each other, or one another. However, when pronounced in another tone, it is a different word and means looks, appearance, bearing posture, or to look at or appraise.

Vacuous comes slow, large,
    and suddenly empty.
Floating, fine, and also soft is soggy.
Scattered is similar to willow flowers with no
    definite track.

Main Diseases Poem

A floating pulse is yang exterior disease
    abiding.
Slow, wind; rapid, heat; tight, cold.
(These are) inflexible.[79]
Floating and has strength, mostly wind heat.
Forceless and also floating is blood vacuity.

Inch floating, headache, vertigo,
    engenderment of wind,
Or one may possibly have wind phlegm
    gathering in the chest.

---

[79] Meaning these indications are definite or certain.

Bar ascending, earth debilitated with
simultaneous wood effulgence.
Within the cubit, urination and defecation not
flowing freely.

SUNKEN PULSE

A sunken pulse is obtained by heavy hand
pressure arriving at the sinews and bones.[80]
It is like thread wrapping sand,
Internally firm, externally soft.
It is like a stone dropped in water.
It must sink to the extreme (*i.e.*, bottom).

Physical Shape Poem
(Like) water moving smoothly below, the pulse
comes sunken,
Between the sinews and bones, soft and
slippery even.

---

[80] This statement comes from the *Mai Jing (Pulse Classic)*.

(For) women (in) the inch, (for) men (in) the
  cubit,
(As long as in) the four seasons the number
  (or size) is level.[81]

Appraising the Types Poem

Sunken, alongside the sinews and bones,
  fitting itself in between.
Deep-lying, find by pushing the sinews and
  touching the bone.
Sunken and fine like thread is truly a weak
  pulse.
Bowstring, long, replete, and large is the
  confined form.

---

[81] As long as the pulse remains normal in number of beats
(and/or size and shape) throughout the four seasons, it is
normal for a woman's pulse to be sunken in the inch and a
man's pulse to be sunken in the cubit.

Main Diseases Poem

Sunken, hidden water amassment, yin channel
disease.

Rapid, heat; slow, cold; slippery, has phlegm.

No force and sunken, vacuity and qi.

Sunken and also has force, accumulation and
also cold.

Inch sunken, phlegm depression, water
collecting in the chest.

Bar, mainly center cold pain not flowing freely.

Cubit position, turbidity, emission, diarrhea
and dysentery,

Kidney vacuity, low back and lower source
similar diseases.

SLOW PULSE

Slow pulse, one respiration, three arrivals.
Departs and comes extremely slowly.[82]

---

[82] This statement comes from the *Mai Jing (Pulse Classic)*.

Physical Shape Poem

Slow comes one respiration only three (beats).

Yang is not overcoming yin, qi,
blood, and/or cold.

If (one) only grasps floating and sunken, (one
can) divide exterior and interior.

The source of dispersing yin must be boosting
fire.

Appraising the Types Poem

A pulse coming (with) three arrival numbers
(*i.e.*, beats) is slow.

A little speedier than slow, moderate (*i.e.*,
relaxed or slightly slow) is grasped.

Slow and fine and difficult to know is choppy.

Floating and also slow and large, vacuity is
inferred.

Main Diseases Poem

Slow commands visceral disease or profuse
phlegm.

Sunken, inveterate concretions and
   conglomerations attentively look for.
Has force and also slow, this is chilly pain.

Slow and also forceless definitely is vacuity
   cold.
Inch slow, must be upper burner cold.
Bar, mainly unendurable center cold pain.
Cubit is kidney vacuity, low back and lower
   leg heaviness,
Urination and defecation not crisp, mounting
   involving the pills (*i.e.*, testicles).

RAPID PULSE

Rapid pulse, one respiration, six arrivals.[83]
The pulse flows, nearly racing.[84]

---

[83] This statement comes from the *Mai Jing (Pulse Classic)*.

[84] This statement comes from the *Su Wen (Simple Questions)*.

Physical Shape Poem

Rapid pulse, between respirations, constantly
  six arrivals.
Yin is faint and yang is exuberant. Must be
  effulgence and vexation.
Floating and sunken, exterior and interior,
  divide vacuity and repletion.
Only in children is this auspicious.

Appraising the Types Poem

Rapid is one more arrival than in a level
  (*i.e.*, normal) person.[85]
Tight comes rapid, pellet-like, and rope-like.
Rapid and sometimes stops is called skipping.
Rapid appearing in the bar center (is) the
  stirring pulse form.

---

[85] Five beats per respiration is normal. Six beats is defined as
rapid.

Main Diseases Poem

Rapid pulse, can know yang heat.
Only take care of sovereign and ministerial
  fires to doctor.

Repletion should be cooled and drained;
  vacuity, warmed and supplemented.
Lung disease autumn, sunken (*i.e.*, difficult).
Step back in fear.

Inch rapid, throat, mouth, tongue sores,
Spitting red, cough, lungs engendering
  abscesses.
Bar, must be stomach fire and liver fire.
Cubit pertains to *Zi Yin Jiang Huo Tang* (Enrich
  Yin & Downbear Fire Decoction).

SLIPPERY PULSE

A slippery pulse goes and comes, advances
  and retreats
Flowingly, uninhibitedly, unfurled, revolving.

It responds to the fingers like a pearl (or bead).[86]

Seeping, seeping as if on the verge of escaping.

Physical Shape & Appraising the Types Poem

The slippery pulse is like feeling a pearl,

Going and coming flowingly and uninhibitedly, retreating yet (always) advancing (again).

Do not take the slippery and rapid as the same type.

The rapid pulse only regards the numbers of arrivals between (respirations).

Main Diseases Poem

The slippery pulse is yang source qi debility,

Phlegm engendering the hundreds of diseases, food engendering disaster.

Above there is vomiting. Below there is amassment of blood.

In a woman's pulse, (whose menses) is regular

---

[86] This statement comes from the *Mai Jing (Pulse Classic)*.

and time is (otherwise) stable, (she) has a fetus.[87]

Inch slippery, diaphragm phlegm engendering
  vomiting,
Swallowing acid, tongue stiff, or possible
cough.
(In) the bar, must be long-standing food,
  liver-spleen heat.
(If there is) thirst, dysentery, bulging[88],
  strangury, look at the cubit position.

---

[87] In other words, if one feels a slippery pulse in a woman whose menses is normally on time but is now overdue, she is probably pregnant (if previously she did not have a slippery pulse and shows no signs of any other pathology which might also cause a slippery pulse).

[88] Bulging means mounting or protrusions in the lower abdomen and inguinal regions.

CHOPPY PULSE

Choppy pulse, fine and slow,
Going and coming difficult,
Short and scattered.
Possibly one stop and again comes.[89]
Uneven, not regular.[90]
Like a light knife scraping bamboo.[91]
Like rain wetting sand.
Like a diseased silkworm eating a leaf.

Physical Shape Poem

Fine, slow, short, (its) going and coming
    difficult.
Scattered, stops. Its yield is sparse. It responds
    to the fingers (as if) thinned out.

---

[89] This description comes from the *Mai Jing (Pulse Classic)*.

[90] This line comes from the *Su Wen (Simple Questions)*.

[91] This simile comes from the *Mai Jue (Pulse Knacks)*.

Like rain wetting sand, its appearance is easily
    scattered.
(Like) a diseased silkworm eating a leaf slowly
    and difficultly.

Appraising the Types Poem

Uneven and irregular is called choppy.
(Like) a light knife scraping bamboo, short and
    difficult.
The faint similarly momentarily prickles, (but)
    the faint is extremely soft.[92]
Floating and sunken is not differentiated and it
    has no spaces.[93]

---

[92] I take momentarily prickling as suddenly speeding up.
However, this line is not perfectly clear to me.

[93] The choppy pulse is like the scattered pulse. However, it
is not floating, while the scattered pulse is. Similarly, it is
somewhat like an intermittent pulse, but it does not actually
skip any beats, "it has no spaces."

Main Diseases Poem

Choppy, therefore the blood is scanty or
essence is damaged.

Contrary stomach (*i.e.*, nausea), perishing yin,
sweat raining and dripping,

Cold dampness entering the constructive
causing blood impediment,

Women's infertility prompted by no
menstruation.

Inch choppy, heart vacuity pain answering
(*i.e.*, radiating) to the chest.

(For) stomach vacuity, rib-side distention,
scrutinize the bar center.

Cubit is essence and blood both damaged
behind,

Intestinal binding, urinary strangury, or
precipitation of red.

VACUOUS PULSE

The vacuous pulse (is) slow, large, and soft.

Press and it is forceless.

Concealed, the fingers suddenly find
emptiness.[94]

Physical Shape & Appraising the Types Poem

Lift and slow and large; press and slack (or
loose).

The pulse shape (has) no margin, like an
empty valley.

Do not grasp the scallion-stalk and vacuous as
one case.[95]

The scallion-stalk comes floating and large
like twisting an onion.

Main Diseases Poem

Pulse vacuous, bodily heat due to damage by
summerheat.

---

[94] This description comes from the *Mai Jing (Pulse Classic)*.

[95] Do not take these two different pulse images as the same.

Spontaneous perspiration, racing heart,
  profuse fright palpitations.
Effusion of heat, yin vacuity, must treat early.
Nourish the constructive, boost the qi.
Do not waste time.

(If) blood is not constructing the heart, the inch
  mouth is vacuous.
Bar center, abdominal distention, eating
  difficult, unhurried (*i.e.*, slow digestion).
Bone-steaming, impediment and wilting,
  damage of essence and blood
Abide in the spirit gate both positions (*i.e.*, on
  both hands).

REPLETE PULSE

The replete pulse is obtained both floating and
  sunken.
The pulse is large and also long,

Slightly bowstring.
It responds to the fingers driving, driving.[96]

Physical Shape Poem

Floating and sunken, large and long are
    obtained in all (depths).
It responds to the fingers without vacuity,
driving, driving, strong.
Heat brewing in the three burners produces
    strong fire.
This is communicated to the intestines. Effuse
    the sweat; only then quiet and healthy.

Appraising the Types Poem

A replete pulse (whether) floating and sunken
    has force and strength.

---

[96] This description comes from the *Mai Jing (Pulse Classic)*.

The tight (pulse) is like a pellet or twisted rope, revolving without taking a side.[97]

One must know that the confined pulse sides with the sinews and bones.

Replete is large and slightly bowstring.

What's more, bandlike and long.

Main Diseases Poem

The replete pulse is yang fire depression and produces

The onset of mania, delirious speech, and repeated spitting (*i.e.*, vomiting).

There may be yang toxins or damage due to food,

Stools not freely flowing, or qi aching.

(If) the inch is replete, correspondingly one knows there is face heat and wind,

---

[97] This line is very difficult to render literally into succinct English. It seems to mean that the tight pulse shakes or vibrates from side to side.

Throat pain, tongue stiffness, qi stuffing the
chest.

Bar, must be spleen heat, central palace
fullness.

Cubit replete, low back or intestine pain not
freely flowing.

LONG PULSE

The long pulse is neither large nor small,
Far, far, calm and at ease.[98]
(If it is) like raising a long rod (with) a thin tip,
it's level (*i.e.*, normal).
(If it is) like a stretched rope (or) like following
a long rod, it's diseased.[99]

---

[98] *Zi ruo* is a compound term which means calm and at ease,
composed, or self-possessed. This description is attributed
to Master Zhu, probably Zhu Dan-xi.

[99] This description comes from the *Su Wen (Simple
Questions).*

Physical Shape & Appraising the Types Poem

A pulse which extends beyond its position is
  called long.
(It) is not only bowstring but full and
  distended.
How to compare the distance of the bowstring
  pulse and long?
A skilled worker certainly (has) the capability
  to measure (these).[100]

Main Diseases Poem

A long pulse, far, far, large, small, evenly
  (divided).
(If) contrary to norm it is diseased, it is like a
  pulled rope.
If no yang toxins (or) withdrawal and mania
  disease,

---

[100] The meaning of measure here is to differentiate the
bowstring from the long. The word I have translated as
measure is literally a cubit measure, *i.e.*, a ruler, which in
English is a noun, not a verb.

Yet there is *yang ming* heat of profound (*i.e.*, great) influence.

SHORT PULSE

A short pulse does not reach its position.[101]
It responds to the fingers (as if) wound up.[102]
It is not able to fill its position.[103]

Physical Shape & Appraising the Types Poem

(If) both heads are contracted, contracted, this is called short.

---

[101] This line comes from the *Mai Jue (Pulse Knack)*.

[102] The Chinese word *hui* shows a box or circle within a box or circle. It means a circle or to wind. It also means to return. It shows something which is closed in on itself and which does not extend outward.

[103] These two lines comes from the *Mai Jing (Pulse Classic)*.

Choppy, short, slow, slow, fine, and difficult.
Short, choppy and also sunken, lung-kidney
     disease,
Or possibly due to qi obstruction or phlegm.

Main Diseases Poem

A short pulse only seen in the cubit and inch,[104]
Short and also slippery and rapid, alcohol
     damaging the spirit.
Floating is blood astringent; sunken is glomus.
Inch, mainly headache. Cubit, abdominal ache.

---

[104] Actually, the pulse is *not* seen in the cubit or inch. Therefore, it is falls short of the cubit and inch.

SURGING PULSE

A surging pulse is extremely large under the
fingers.[105]
It comes exuberant and departs debilitated.[106]
Comes large; goes long.

Physical Shape Poem

The pulse comes surging and exuberant
and departs and goes debilitated.
It fills the fingers, flooding, flooding.
It corresponds to the summer time.
If in the spring, fall, or winter, (*i.e.,*) yin
divisions,
Upbearing yang, scattering fire do not doubt.

---

[105] This description comes from the *Mai Jing (Pulse Classic)*.

[106] This line comes from the *Su Wen (Simple Questions)*.

Appraising the Types Poem

Surging comes beating, beating, suddenly.
It departs debilitated but comes exuberant
 like billows (or great waves).
(If) one wishes to know how to handle the
 difference (between it and) the replete pulse,
Lifting and pressing, it is bowstring, long,
 driving, driving, and hard.

Main Diseases Poem

Pulse surging, yang exuberance, blood
 correspondingly vacuous,

Fire and heat flaming and flaring, heat disease
 abiding,
Distention and fullness, stomach turned over.
Must treat early.
Yin vacuity, diarrhea and dysentery.
How can one hesitate?

Inch surging, heart fire, upper burner flaring.

When the lung pulse (is) surging, metal cannot
   endure.
(For) liver fire, stomach vacuity, scrutinize in
   the bar.
(For) kidney vacuity, yin fire, look in the cubit.

FAINT PULSE

The faint pulse is extremely fine and soft.
Press and it is as if on the verge of expiring.
May have, may not.[107]
Fine with a thin tip and long.[108]

---

[107] This means that sometimes you feel the pulse and
sometimes you don't. It is so fine and forceless, it is easy to
lose. This description comes from the *Mai Jing (Pulse Classic)*.

[108] *I.e.*, very attenuated

Physical Shape & Appraising the Types Poem

Faint pulse, soft, faint, so worn, so worn.
Press and it is as if on the verge of expiring.
Have, then don't.
Faint is yang weakness. Fine, yin weakness.
Fine and faint are quite similar in width.

Main Diseases Poem

The qi and blood (are) faint, so also the pulse is
    faint.
Aversion to cold, effusion of heat, sweat
    dribbling and dripping.
In males, this is due to extreme taxation and all
    are vacuity indications.
In females, there is flooding and *dai xia* disease.

Inch faint, qi (*i.e.*, breathing) hurried or heart
    palpitations.
When the bar pulse faint, distended, full form.
(When) seen in the cubit position, this is
    essence blood weakness,

Aversion to cold, wasting, jaundice, pain, moaning and groaning.

TIGHT PULSE

The tight pulse comes and goes with force.
Left and right, pellet-like to the human hand.[109]
Like a twisted string, not constant.[110]
Rapid, like a pressing rope.[111]
Like the twine knitting a raft.[112]

---

[109] These first lines comes from the *Su Wen (Simple Questions)*.

[110] Not constant means vibrating from side to side. This description is attributed to (Zhang) Zhong-jing. That means it is from the *Shan Han Lun (Treatise on Damage [Due to] Cold)*.

[111] This line comes from the *Mai Jing (Pulse Classic)*.

[112] This simile is from (Zhu) Dan-xi.

Physical Shape Poem

Press, like a twisted strong. Pressing like rope.
The pulse image, therefore,
has obtained the name tight.
Invariably, it is (due to) cold evils coming and
    invading.
Internally, it makes abdominal pain, externally,
    body aches.

Main Diseases Poem

Tight is mainly all pain due to cold,
Panting and coughing, wind epilepsy, spitting
    chilly phlegm.
Floating and tight, exterior cold.
Must emit and effuse.
Tight and sunken, warm and scatter.
Naturally quiet.
Inch tight, human prognosis and qi mouth
    divide.
Just at bar, heart and abdominal pain very
    heavy.

Within the cubit have tight, this is yin chill.
There must be running piglet or mounting
  ache.

MODERATE (*I.E.*, RELAXED) PULSE

The moderate pulse departs and comes a little
  faster than the slow.[113]
One respiration, four arrivals.
Like silk in the warp,
It is not swept along its spool.
It responds to the fingers harmonious and
  moderate,
Going and coming very evenly.[114]
Like the image of willows dancing in the wind
  at the beginning of spring.[115]

---

[113] This description comes from the *Mai Jing (Pulse Classic)*.

[114] This description is attributed to Zhang Tai-su.

[115] This description is attributed to Yang Xuan-cao.

Like a faint wind softly picking up the tips of
the willows.[116]

Physical Shape Poem

The moderate pulse, sigh, sigh, four arrivals
notify,
(Like) willow tips waving, waving, picked up
by soft wind.
Leisurely passing through the vessels interior,
seek the spirit qi.
Even if joined with other guests, harmonious
and moderate are in the midst.[117]

Main Diseases Poem

Moderate pulse, constructive debilitated,
defensive has a surplus.

---

[116] This description is attributed to Hua Bo-ren.

[117] The moderate pulse indicates having spirit qi. Even if
there are other pulse images, as long as the moderate pulse
is mixed in with these, there is spirit qi.

Possible wind, possible dampness, possible
   spleen vacuity.
Above is stiff neck; below, wilting and
   impediment.
Divide and differentiate the categories of
   floating and sunken, large and small.
Inch moderate, wind evils neck and upper
   back inflexible.
Bar is wind vertigo, stomach household
   vacuity.
Spirit gate, wet diarrhea or wind constipation.
Or it may be limping, foot power dissipated.[118]

---

[118] Literally, the last word in this line means roundabout,
circuitous, or winding. However, that is not very
meaningful when combined with the preceding two words.
There is four word compound term, *yu yu tang tang*, which
means lounging or dissipated. This does make sense here.
In that case, this one word may be an allusion to that four
word compound term. Unfortunately, my Chinese is not
good enough to know this for sure.

SCALLION-STALK PULSE

The scallion-stalk pulse is floating, large, and
    also soft.
Press and its center is empty (or hollow).
Both side are replete.[119]
Center is empty, external is replete (or real, *i.e.*,
    exists).
Its shape is like an onion stalk.

Physical Shape Poem

Scallion-stalk form, floating, large, soft, onion
    stalk.
Press and it has sides. Center is empty.
Fire attacking the yang channels; blood
    ascends and spills over.
Heat assails the yin network vessels; below
    flows red.

---

[119] This description comes from the *Mai Jing (Pulse Classic)*.

Appraising the Types Poem

Center empty, sides real is scallion-stalk.

Floating, large, and also slow is called the
vacuous pulse.

Scallion-stalk but also bowstring is called
drumskin.

Scallion-stalk is blood collapse. Drumskin is
blood vacuity.

Main Diseases Poem

Inch scallion-stalk, accumulation of blood in
the chest.

In the bar meet the scallion-stalk, intestinal and
stomach abscess.

(If it) appears in the cubit position, mostly
precipitation of blood.

Red strangury, red dysentery, leaking and
flooding.

BOWSTRING PULSE

The bowstring pulse is level and straight like
   the long.[120]
It is like a drawn bowstring.[121]
Press and it does not vary.
Pluck, pluck, like pressing the strings of a
   dulcimer.[122]
Its shape is like the strings of a zither.[123]
Passing through, straight and continuous,
It is stiff under the fingers.

---

[120] This description comes from the *Su Wen (Simple
Questions)*.

[121] This simile comes from the *Mai Jing (Pulse Classic)*.

[122] These two lines are attributed to Master Cao, *i.e.*, Cao
Yuan-fang, the author of the *Zhu Bing Yuan Hou Lun
(Treatise on the Causes & Symptoms of All Diseases)*. Pluck,
pluck actually mean to press, press, not literally to pluck.

[123] This simile comes from the *Mai Jue (Pulse Knack)*.

Physical Shape Poem

Bowstring pulse, on and on, level, straight, and
 long.
Liver channel wood effulgent.
Earth, correspondingly, is damaged.
Angry qi, fullness in the chest, constant desire
 to sigh,
(Eye) screen, clouded pupils, tears dripping
 and drenching.

Appraising the Types Poem

Bowstring come level and straight like the
 string of a bow.
Tight is like a rope, left and right pellet-like.
Tight bespeaks of its strength. Bowstring
 bespeaks of its image (or shape).
The confined pulse is bowstring, long, and
 sunken or deep-lying.

Main Diseases Poem

Bowstring corresponds to the east, the liver
 and gallbladder channels,

Rheum and phlegm, cold and heat, malaria,
and entwined body.

Floating and sunken, slow and rapid, must be
differentiated.

(Likewise,) large and small, one or both, heavy
and light.

Inch bowstring, head pain, diaphragm profuse
phlegm.

(For) cold and heat, concretions and
conglomerations, scrutinize the left bar.

The right bar, stomach cold, heart and
abdominal pain.

Within the cubit, yin mounting, lower leg
hypertonicity.

DRUMSKIN PULSE

Drumskin pulse, bowstring and scallion-
stalk.[124]
Like pressing the skin of a drum.[125]

Physical Shape & Main Diseases Poem

The drumskin pulse, its form is like pressing
the skin of a drum,
Scallion-stalk and bowstring mutually combine
(in this) pulse (of) cold vacuity.
(In) females, half birth[126] and flooding and
leaking.
(In) males, constructive vacuity or dream
emission.

---

[124] This description is attributed to (Zhang) Zhong-jing.

[125] This simile is attributed to (Zhu) Dan-xi.

[126] *I.e.*, miscarriage

CONFINED PULSE

The confined pulse is similar to sunken, similar
   to deep-lying.
(But it is) replete, large, and also long,
Slightly bowstring.[127]

Physical Shape & Appraising the Types Poem

Bowstring, long, replete, and large, are
   similarly hard like the confined.
(But) the confined position abides constantly
   sunken and deep-lying.
The drumskin pulse is scallion-stalk and
   bowstring, but self(-evidently) floats and
   rises.
The drumskin is vacuous. The confined is
   replete. This essential (should be) clearly
   known and minded.

---

[127] This description comes from the *Mai Jing (Pulse Classic)*.

Main Diseases Poem

Cold leads to confined and hard.

The interior has a surplus.

Abdominal and heart cold pain, wood
attacking the spleen.

Mounting, concretions and conglomerations,
what distress!

Loss of blood, yin vacuity. Step back in dread.

SOGGY PULSE

The soggy pulse is extremely soft as well as
floating and fine.

It is like a thread in water.

A light hand and it can be obtained.

Press and no have.[128]

Like a bubble floating on top of water.

---

[128] This description comes from the *Mai Jing (Pulse Classic)*.

Physical Shape Poem

The soggy form is floating and fine.
Pressing must be light.
It is like a thread floating on the (sur)face of
    water. Force it cannot bear.
After disease or birthing, (if) it fits exactly,
    there are medicinals.[129]
(If this pulse) appears in a level (or normal)
    person, there is no root.

Appraising the Types Poem

Floating as well as soft and fine is known as
    soggy.
Sunken, fine, and soft oppositely makes weak.
Faint is floating and faint as if on the verge of
    expiry.
Fine comes sunken.
Fine is closely related to faint.

---

[129] This exceptionally terse line means that, after serious or
long disease or childbirth, if the pulse and symptoms (of
vacuity) match each other, there are medicinals which can
(easily) treat this.

Main Diseases Poem

Soggy is blood collapse, yin vacuity disease.
The sea of marrow and field of cinnabar are
    darkly already depleted.[130]
Sweat rains at night mixed with steaming of
    the bones.
Blood mounts, flooding invertedly.[131]
Dampness assails the spleen.

Inch soggy, yang faint, spontaneous
    perspiration profuse.
In the bar, how can the qi not be vacuous?
Cubit, damaged essence, blood vacuity, severe
    cold.
Warming and supplementing true yin can lift
    the illness.

---

[130] I believe darkly here refers to secretly or inwardly, *i.e.*,
internally.

[131] Inverted flooding refers to vicarious menstruation,
menstruation occurring from an orifice other than the
vagina. This often occurs from the nose or stomach/throat.

107

WEAK PULSE

The weak pulse is extremely soft as well as
    sunken and fine.
Press and you obtain it.
Lift the hand and no have.[132]

Physical Shape Poem

Weak come without force. Press it softly.
Soft and fine and also sunken, it does not ap-
    pear floating.
Yang fall entering yin, essence blood
    weakness.
White head, still. Less years, can worry.[133]

---

[132] This description comes from the *Mai Jing (Pulse Classic)*.

[133] This is another exceedingly terse line. It means that, if one
feels a weak pulse in an old person, they still can live or
they will live on yet. But, if one feels this pulse in one of few
years, this can rightly be a cause for worry.

Main Diseases Poem

Weak pulse, yin vacuity, yang qi debility,
Aversion to cold, effusion of heat, sinews and
bone wilting,
Profuse palpitations, profuse sweating, essence
spirit decreased.
Boost the qi and regulate the constructive.
Take care to doctor early.
Inch weak, yang vacuity disease can be known.
Bar is stomach weakness or spleen debility.
On the verge of yang fall, yin vacuity disease,
Must grasp both spirit gate positions to infer.

SCATTERED PULSE

The scattered pulse is large and scattered.
It has an exterior but no interior.[134]
Its edges are scattered and not restrained.
No pulling together discipline.[135]
No restraint.
It arrives scattered without being together.
Or it may come many and depart few.
It may depart many and come few.
Its edges are scattered and no restrained
Like the image of willow flowers scattered all
over the place.

Physical Shape Poem

Scattered is similar to the image of willow
flowers scattered all over, flying.[136]
Departs and comes without definitude.

---

[134] This description comes from the *Mai Jing (Pulse Classic)*.

[135] *Jie* means a node or divider and, therefore, by extension, discipline. Here it implies edges.

[136] Flying, *i.e.*, fluttering in the air.

Arrives with difficult togetherness.

(During) birthing, it's life. (During) a
    threatened miscarriage, it's falling.

If come upon in enduring disease, emergency
    quickly doctor.

Appraising the Types Poem

The scattered pulse is not constrained.

It's scattered all over the place.

Soggy comes floating and fine (like) thread in
    water.

Floating and also slow and large is the vacuous
    pulse.

Scallion-stalk is empty in the center but has
    two edges.

Main Diseases Poem

Left inch, heart racing. Right inch, sweating.

Spilling rheum, the left bar is correspondingly
    soft and scattered.

Right bar soft and scattered, back of foot swelling.

(If) scattered abides in both cubits, the ethereal
    soul has correspondingly been cut off.

FINE PULSE

The fine pulse is small, but larger than faint.
It also is constantly there.
Fine, straight, and also soft.
It responds to the fingers like a silk thread.[137]

Physical Shape Poem

Fine comes gaunt like silk.
It responds to the fingers sunken, sunken, but
   is not severed.[138]
In spring and summer or (in those of) few
   years, these are not favorable.
In fall and winter or in the aged and weak,
   these are mutually appropriate.

---

[137] This description comes from the *Mai Jing (Pulse Classic)*.

[138] In other words, no matter how deeply one pushes, the fine pulse does not disappear or is not cut off by heavy pressure.

Main Diseases Poem

The fine pulse, fringe, fringe, blood and qi
     debility.
All vacuous, taxation, detriment, attack by the
     seven affects.
If no damp qi is assailing the low back and
     kidneys,
Yet there is damaged essence with sweating
     and discharge next.

Inch fine, correspondingly know there is
     repeated vomiting.
In the bar, abdominal distention, stomach
     vacuity, and form (vacuity).[139]
(If) meet in the cubit, certainly there is cinnabar
     field chill,
Diarrhea and dysentery, emission of essence,
     any desertion of yin.

---

[139] The last three words in this line literally read stomach
vacuity form. I believe this means there is stomach vacuity
and vacuous form or, in other words, emaciation.

DEEP-LYING PULSE

The deep-lying pulse, heavy pressure, look to the bone.

Beneath the fingers, one is capable (of feeling) stirring.[140]

The pulse moves under the sinews.

Physical Shape Poem

The deep-lying pulse, push the sinews and search to the bone.

In the space between the fingers (and the bone), there is the capability of stirring, but lurking very deep.

Damage (due to) cold on the verge of sweating, yang is about to resolve.

Reversal counterflow, navel pain patterns categorized as yin.

---

[140] This description comes from the *Mai Jing (Pulse Classic)*.

Main Diseases Poem

Deep-lying is sudden turmoil[141], repeated
   vomiting,
Abdominal pain, profuse climbing (*i.e.*,
   vomiting), long-standing food collecting,
Amassment of rheum and old phlegm
   producing accumulations and gatherings.
Scatter cold, warm the interior.
(Then) there is no cause for abiding.

(If there is) food depression within the chest,
   both inches will be deep-lying,
A desire to spit up, but not spitting up,
   constantly rising, rising.
(In the) bar, there must be abdominal pain on
   the basis of sunken, sunken.
Behind the bar, mounting aching as if the
   abdomen would split.

---

[141] Sudden turmoil means cholera-like diseases characterized
by severe, repeated vomiting and diarrhea.

STIRRING PULSE

The stirring is a rapid pulse seen in the bar.
Above and below, no head or tail[142],
Large as a bean,
It stirs and shakes (or waves).

Physical Shape Poem

The stirring pulse is shaking, shaking, rapid,
    and located in the bar.
No head, no tail, bean-like in form.
Its origin and root is yin and yang wrestling.

---

[142] Contemporary Chinese versions and commentaries tend to punctuate and explain this stanza differently. In that case, the first line reads: "The scattered is a rapid pulse seen in the bar, above, *and* below." If translated this way, this pulse image might appear in any of the three positions. However, Li says in the Physical Shape Poem below that this pulse is located in the bar, and later, in the Main Diseases Poem, he gives no discrimination of indications by inch, bar, and cubit.

The vacuous (*i.e.*, the loser) is shaking, while
the victor is quiet.

Main Diseases Poem

The stirring pulse monopolizes and commands
pain and fright,
Sweating due to yang stirring, heat affecting
yin.
Or there may be diarrhea and dysentery and
hypertonicity disease.
In males, collapse of essence.
In females, flooding.

SKIPPING PULSE

The skipping pulse comes and departs rapidly.
Sometimes it stops once and then again
    comes.[143]
It is like stumbling while hurrying.
Slower (than) racing, not constant (*i.e.,*
    interrupted).

Physical Shape Poem

Skipping pulse is rapid and also sometime
    stops once.
It is extreme yang, on the verge of yin collapse.
Triple burner depressive fire flaring, flaming,
    and exuberant.
(If) it advances, it must be no life.
(If) it follows, can live.[144]

---

[143] This description comes from the *Mai Jing (Pulse Classic)*.

[144] According to Chinese commentaries, advancing means
the skipped beats becoming more frequent and the intervals
within the skips becoming longer. Following or retreating
means less and shorter skips.

Main Diseases Poem

The skipping pulse is only incited by fire
   disease.

Its causes are five. Finely grind (or
   differentiate) these.

From time to time, (there is) panting and

coughing and all kinds of phlegm
   accumulation.

Its (also) possible (to have) onset of mania,
   macules, and toxic flat abscesses.

BOUND PULSE

The bound pulse goes and comes moderate
(*i.e.,* relaxed or slightly slow).
Sometimes it stops once and then comes
again.[145]

Physical Shape Form

The bound pulse is moderate (or relaxed) and
also sometimes stops once.
Sole yin is predominately exuberant.
Yang is on the verge of collapsing.
Floating is qi stagnation. Sunken is accumulation.
A clear division of sweating and precipitating
is advocated.

Main Diseases Poem

The bound pulse is always due to qi and blood
congelation.

---

[145] This description comes from the *Mai Jing (Pulse Classic)*.

Old phlegm is bound and stagnates (with) bitterness and profound moaning (*i.e.,* intense pain).

Internally are engendered accumulation and gathering. Externally are welling abscesses and swelling.

Mounting and concretions are calamitous diseases categorized as yin.

REGULARLY INTERRUPTED PULSE

The regularly interrupted pulse, its stirring has with stops within it.

It is not able to return by itself.

Due to a cause, it stirs again.[146]

The pulse arrival retreats to the cubit.

(After) a very long time, (it resumes its) direction again.

---

[146] This description comes from the (Zhang) Zhong-jing.

Physical Shape Poem

It stirring has stops within it.
It is not able to return.
It stirs again due (to some cause).
This is why it is regarded as interrupted.
Obtained in all those with disease, (it's)
    worrisome but can be treated.
In a level (or normal) person, stepping back
    and longevity are mutually close.[147]

Appraising the Types Poem

Rapid and sometimes stops is called skipping.
Moderate (or relaxed) and stopping must be
    taken as the bound pulse.

---

[147] This means that, when this pulse image is felt in an otherwise normal person, one should be very careful. Otherwise, this person's longevity is in jeopardy. This makes sense, since this pulse is associated with serious heart disease. Patients with this pulse image should be referred to an MD or ER unless they are under current physician care for a heart condition.

If it stops and is not able to return to its
    position, this is regularly interrupted.
Bound, life; regularly interrupted, death.
Different routes.

Main Diseases Poem

The regularly interrupted pulse has its original
    cause in visceral qi debility.
Abdominal pain, diarrhea and dysentery,
    lower source depletion.
Possibly there is vomiting and diarrhea, central
    palace disease.
(In) women, the fetus has been cherished for
    three months.

BIBLIOGRAPHY

Chinese Language Bibliography

Bin Hu Mai Xue Bai Shou Jie (A Clear Explanation of the Lakeside Master's Study of the Pulse) by the Beijing College of Traditional Chinese Medicine, People's Health & Hygiene Press, Beijing, 1993

Lu Shan Tang Lei Bian (Lu Mountain Hall Discrimination of Categories) by Zhang Zhi-cong, Jiangsu Science & Technology Press, 1982

Mai Jing (Pulse Classic) by Wang Shu-he, Peoples' Health & Hygiene Press, Beijing, 1982

Mai Jing Xiao Shi (A School Explanation of the Pulse Classic) by Fuzhou Municipal Peoples' Hospital, Peoples' Health & Hygiene Press, Beijing, 1984

Mai Xue Xin Shou (Heart Sayings in the Study of the Pulse) by Li Shi-Mao & Tian Shu-xiao, Chinese Medicine Ancient Books Press, Beijing, 1994

Se Mai She Zhen (Color, Pulse & Tongue Examination) by Wu Han-xiang, Shanghai Science & Technology Press, Shanghai, 1987

Si Zhen Jue Wei (Picking Out the Profundities of the Four Examinations) by Lin Zhi-han, Tianjin Science & Technology Publishing House, Tianjin, 1993

Yi Xue Chuan Xin Lu (Record Transmitting the Heart of the Study of Medicine) by Liu Yi-ren, Hebei People's Press, Tangshan, 1977

Yi Zong Jin Jian (Golden Mirror of Ancestral Medicine) ed. by Wu Qian, People's Health & Hygiene Press, Beijing, 1985

Zhong Guo Yi Xue Zhen Fa Da Quan (A Great, Complete [Compendium] of Methods of Medical Examination in China) by Ma Zhong-xue, Shandong Science & Technology Press, Jinan, 1991

Zhong Yi Mai Xue Ru Men (Entering the Gate of the Study of the Pulse in Chinese Medicine) by Jiang Chang-yuan, Science & Technology Literary Press, Chengdu, Sichuan, 1986

Zhong Yi Mai Xue San Zi Jue (Three Character Rhymes in the Study of the Pulse in Chinese Medicine) by Xiao Jin-shun, People's Army Press, Beijing, 1995

Zhong Yi Mai Zhen Xue (A Study of Chinese Medicine's Pulse Examination) by Zhao En-jian, Tianjing Science & Technology Press, Tianjin, 1995

Zhong Yi Ru Men (Entering the Gate of Chinese Medicine) by Qin Bo-wei, contained in Paul U. Unschuld's *Learn to Read Chinese, Vol. 1*, Paradigm Publications, Brookline, MA, 1994

Zhong Yi Wu Zi Jing (Chinese Medicine Five Character Classic) by Liu Ying-zhong, Chinese National Chinese Medicine & Medicinals Press, Beijing, 1993

Zhong Yi Zhen Duan Xue (A Study of Chinese Medical Diagnosis) by Deng Tie-tao, People's Health & Hygiene Press, Beijing, 1994

Zhong Yi Zhen Duan Xue Jie (Explanation of Chinese Medical Diagnosis) by Ji Feng-xia & Zhou Yu-long, TCM Ancient Literature Press, Beijing, 1986

Chinese-English Bibliography

Chinese-English Terminology of Traditional Chinese Medicine by Shuai Xue-zhong, Hunan Science & Technology Press, Changsha, 1983

English-Chinese Chinese-English Dictionary of Chinese Medicine by Nigel Wiseman, Hunan Science & Technology Press, Changsha, 1995

English Language Bibliography

Chin Kuei Yao Lueh (Prescriptions from the Golden Chamber) by Zhang Zhong-jing, trans. by Wang Su-yen & Hong-yen Hsu, Oriental Healing Arts Institute, Los Angeles, CA, 1983

The Essential Book of Traditional Chinese Medicine, Vol. 1, Theory by Liu Yanchi, Columbia University Press, NY, 1988

The Essentials of Chinese Diagnostics by Manfred Porkert, Chinese Medicine Publications Inc., Zurich, Switzerland, 1983

Extra Treatises Based on Investigation & Inquiry by Zhu Dan-xi, trans. by Yang Shou-zhong & Duan Wu-jin, Blue Poppy Press, Boulder, CO, 1994

Fundamentals of Chinese Medicine, a compilation of texts from the Beijing, Nanjing, and Shanghai Colleges of TCM, trans. by Nigel Wiseman & Andy Ellis, Paradigm Publications, Brookline, MA, 1985

Li Dong-yuan's Treatise on the Spleen & Stomach by Li Dong-yuan, trans. by Yang Shou-zhong & Li Jian-yong, Blue Poppy Press, Boulder, CO, 1993

Master Hua's Classic of the Central Viscera by Hua Tuo, trans. by Yang Shou-zhong, Blue Poppy Press, Boulder, CO, 1993

Nan Ching (The Classic of Difficult Issues), trans. by Paul U. Unschuld, University of California Press, Berkeley, CA, 1986

Pulse Diagnosis by Li Shi-zhen, trans. by Hoc Ku Hyunh, Paradigm Publications, Brookline, MA, 1981. (In actuality, this is not a translation of the *Bin Hu Mai Xue [The Lakeside Master's Study of the Pulse]* by Li Shi-zhen and his father but a translation of the commentary on that book appearing in *Zhong Yi Mai Xue Ru Men* cited above.)

Shang Han Lun, The Great Classic of Chinese Medicine by Zhang Zhong-jing, trans. by Hong-yen Hsu & William G. Peacher, Oriental Healing Arts Institute, Los Angeles, CA, 1981

The Pulse Classic, A Translation of Wang Shu-he's Mai Jing, trans. by Yang Shou-zhong, Blue Poppy Press, Boulder, CO, 1997

Traditional Medicine in Contemporary China by Nathan Sivin, Center for Chinese Studies, University of Michigan, Ann Arbor, MI, 1987. This is a partial translation of *Xin Pian Zhong Yi Xue Kai Yao (Revised Outline of Chinese Medicine)*.

The Web That Has No Weaver: Understanding Chinese Medicine by Ted Kaptchuk, Congdon & Weed, NY, 1983